A PROLIFIC PRAYER

Brandon Tyrelle Chambers

A Prolific Prayer

Brandon Tyrelle Chambers
All rights reserved.
ISBN: 979-8-218-39501-8

Book Design: Williams DocuPrep
www.williamsdocuprep.com

Dedication

Sincerely, I dedicate this book, *"A Prolific Prayer"* to my beloved father "George Thomas Chambers" and my much-loved mother, Janice Mcduffie Chambers. I specifically dedicate this book to my father due to how he planted the encouragement to achieve a life completely full of love, joy and peace. While on the other hand, I dedicate this book to my mother as well due to how she successfully planted the idea of faith within, as a solution of prayer for the means of achieving a blessed life of peace.

Contents

Acknowledgments

With deepest gratitude, I sincerely acknowledge the great help of my mother, Janice Mcduffie Chambers, who helped provide me with the needed material to achieve my goal of successfully writing "A Prolific Prayer." Also, with great appreciation, I would like to acknowledge Angeline Williams of Williams DocuPrep, who helped me get this book published in my need of a compassionate publisher.

Preface

In 2020, my life seemed to collapse nearly completely. Circumstances brought me to the point of distress and despair. As friends, family, and my freedom slowly began to fade away, I felt like I was losing everything I had affection for. Yet, as a result of my unfortunate circumstances, one day the life predicament that I was dealing with just so happened to grow so heavy upon me that I was pressed into a prayer of complete supplication.

Now, even though I am a pastor's son who had a sound experience with an idea of God, truthfully, at that moment, I wasn't even sure who I was praying to. The reason being that, specifically during that time of my life, I honestly had lost all belief in the particular faith that I once had.

However, I can clearly remember unloading the burden of pressure against the breath of my soul as I humbly confessed the issue I was dealing with, praying for a great change. For instance, I prayed earnestly to whatever was responsible for my soul's existence and prayed for it to build me into the fullness of my purpose and to somehow fill me with a knowledge that would powerfully manifest the accomplishment of a prolific rest pertaining to the complete joy and peace I was desperately yearning for.

Over time, I gradually acknowledged many concepts of knowledge that made me feel as if I had found a structure of purpose. Yet, in return, the knowledge of many of those structures only proved to fail me, as it in some way led me back into the frustrating experience of misery and disappointment. Nevertheless, throughout all of my falls, I still came to learn certain perceptions of a particular knowledge that innocently proved to manifest a sincere, stable joy upon the breath of my soul.

Nevertheless, I was still in a great windstorm of despair, and on top of that, things certainly didn't seem to get better once my beloved father passed away in late 2021. In fact, it grew worse as depression attacked my soul even more. I was already battling one great unfortunate circumstance within another, and consequently, I spent many nights in pain, crying even more due to how my father was the absolute closest affection that I held within my heart, next to very few others.

However, while experiencing the turmoil of even more distress, disappointment, and the mental effects of sorrow, I constantly thought back on the relationship that my father and I shared. I thought about how we both experienced great dysfunction within our family that happened to lead to many traumatizing situations of dissension, slander, and complete loss of peace.

I thought about how many times I walked in on my father stretched out on his bed in complete despair about the inevitable challenges of frustration, unhappiness, and forms of war that life had brought him. I thought about how I would uplift my father, get him out of the depths of the feeling he was experiencing, and, in some way, help my father find joy once again.

It troubled me to hear of my father's situation before he passed away. Specifically of all the hatred and spite he dealt with in his needed time of love. Yet in return, these pains of sorrow that I'd buried consequently began to sprout a profound interest within to amplify the love that I had for my father. It inspired me with an interest to turn that same love into a service to the world as a newly discovered purpose in life.

Gradually, my heart began to be purged from all of the deceitful knowledge of behavior that had only brought the disturbance of sorrow into my life. Then I began to slowly recognize a structure of knowledge that produced an emotional state of complete joy and peace. It was pure, with no dissension, and simple and without any burdening religious standards. Most of all, it was fulfilling as it emanated the awareness of a purpose, a wisdom, and a result of complete rest within absolute happiness and peace.

I grew to see this structure of knowledge as an indestructible fit pertaining to the description of a Supreme Spirit, which is a supreme mental arrangement for an uncomplicating success of absolute joy. Therefore, as a prolific outcome of my experience of getting to know this Supreme Structure of Knowledge, I wrote this book, "A Prolific Prayer," to share an innocent, indestructible, and successful structure of knowledge to intentionally spread the self-proven source of all true eternal joy and peace.

So surely, "A Prolific Prayer" is a mere description of my perceived view of God, as in my envisioned image of a complete and perfect structure of knowledge for the sound outcome of absolute joy and peace. Furthermore, as the profound treasure of my soul, "A Prolific Prayer" is my purpose-filled present towards the world as a service to excite the complete health of an indestructible peace for a yearning soul.

Therefore, with that being said, I hope you enjoy conceiving the knowledge-filled fruit of "A Prolific Prayer" and, in return, find complete healing upon your soul as you find a complete mental source of life manifesting knowledge.

Quiet Prayer

The Lord God formed the man from the soil of the ground and breathed into his nostrils the breath of life, and the man became a living creature. — Genesis 2:7

The moment I truly acknowledged this Scripture, I instantly became fascinated with breath. Now I know it may sound odd to some, but to be more specific, it interested me as I grew to see the operation of breathing as an actual act of quiet prayer. For instance, to define the act of praying specifically, it is to earnestly seek the essentials of joy, happiness, and peace.

Just as it is in the same manner as the operation of breathing.

To specify, the operation of breathing is typically the draw of seeking for the essentials of life by the act of an inhale in order to live and experience the exhale of a peaceful rest. Therefore, wouldn't you think that life is also of the same manner? For example, in the cycle of our lives, accordingly, we would be presented with circumstances of which we would be obligated to receive the right essentials of life in order to overcome the obstacles and achieve a prolific rest.

However, throughout my experience of life, I also had to learn that there is a mass majority of breaths among the earth that lack the prolificity of rest. In other words, there are many souls that are left without the resting exhale of an achieved peace. Why is this so? Well, to illustrate, it is because of the time that they have spent in their lives they have lived an unprolific prayer that, accordingly, never supplied their seek for the salvation of life, with the satisfaction of rest.

Therefore, their lives had become an uneasy experience of an unhappy, discontent, and desperate search for the fulfillment of life's struggle for joy and peace. Just as how my life was before I found the path of prayer that led me to the accomplishment of prolification.

You may wonder what I mean by "prolific." My meaning of a prolific prayer is to achieve an abundant outcome of peace, which is the complete achieved nature of life. That which, accordingly, leaves behind an inspirational legacy of testimonial fruits that fulfill the soul with the accomplishment of valuably presenting the enlightened path of an intellectual prayer.

So nevertheless the breath of our souls is only the beginning of achieving a prolific prayer. Yet as we all live a life of some sort of prayer, the achievement a prolific prayer can only come when the soul is fed the revealing principles of an infinite, indestructible, and truthful notion of life. Therefore, as a fruit of my proliferation, I aim to share that notion of life with you.

Supplication

To begin my illustration, I would like to share with you my experience of how I achieved prolific prayer. It started with me experiencing a common issue that presses against many souls on earth, which is the constant presence of frustration and misery in my life.

Through the pains I acquired from my miserable circumstances, the natural cry of my soul amplified to a desperate desire for life. The breath of my life seemed to have sunk so deeply into the depths of misery that I had come to the point where I was humbled into a forced meditation so I could finally hear the solution for my reoccurring misery. Through the humbling of my spirit, I gracefully grew to recognize that every turmoil that I was experiencing was in some way a result of me abiding affectionately by a foolish aspect.

I started to realize that the lifestyle of pain and misery I was living was simply a manifestation of the state of my mind. I gradually found myself aligning my heart with the breathing desire of my soul for life. Once a renewal of my mind began to take place, I grew to see who God is.

I sensed God's instructing commands for the internal feeling of complete joy and peace. By acknowledging God's instruction, I grew to understand that the pains of my soul were surely the chastising call for me to seek the clarity of the Divine Spirit that blew my soul into creation.

As I humbly submitted to prayer, I increasingly began to see a clear image of who God is. My spirit became flooded with the revealing light of God. Then it appeared to me that the essence of God was a body of principles that essentially formed the supreme spirit that birthed the nature of peace and the blessed state of life, which all souls naturally yearned for.

So, by the humble observation of God's character, it was then that I began to perceive the principles of God's Spirit, which appeared to me in the fashion of a fundamental sequence that suitably from the first principle of God's Spirit. The rest would evolve, so on and so on.

The appearance of God illuminated to me as the principles of characteristics that form the essence of God's Spirit revealed to be as the face of God. Therefore, at the beginning of my next chapter, I would like to reveal to you the empowering character of God.

The Face of God

To begin illustrating the face of God I would first like to explain my purpose for why I proclaim this revelation to be the face of God. The face defines the principal surface of anything. That is the receiving of the subject's ethical behavior. So therefore, as the face of God these revealed principles exposed the affectionate faith of God's ethical behavior for the prolific achievement of the complete emotional health of life's joy, and peace.

The Principles of God's Character

1. Majestic Nature of Dignity

To specify the perceived principles of God's life manifesting character, I first came to recognize God's character trait of a majestic nature, which is the nature of a dignified manner. From this first empowering fundamental trait I perceived the education of God's belief of thoughtfully behaving in a manner of cautiously avoiding the cause of misery among thine own self.

In other words, it is in the sense of carefully protecting the manifested peace of thine own spirit. Therefore, we can conclude that it is the trait of intentionally avoiding the manner of foolishness that would cause the shameful defilement of regret.

2. Purity

Next, because of the completely developed will of the majestic nature of dignity, it appeared to me that God's second trait evolved from the concept of His trait of dignity. As a result, the next principle of God evolved to be a principle of purity. This educating character trait of God accordingly revealed to me God's will of intentionally not being the cause of any misery arousing outside of His own Spirit.

In other words, having the character trait of possessing an aspect to cautiously not arouse the nature of misery by all and anything done by His spirit. This trait inspired me with the perception of intentionally not causing any arousal of misery by any exaltation done by my spirit. Specifically for the means of achieving the stability of peace in my life while also avoiding the burdening development of guilt.

3. Immeasurable Mind

Once I became fully aware of God's complete trait of purity, God's next characteristic began to unfold. It revealed to me that by the fundamental growth of God Character, God Spirit develops the trait of possessing an Immeasurable Mind. That is, the principle that reveals the immeasurable belief that the achievement of peace and life is certain to be achieved by the faith of God's Principles of dignity and purity.

As this empowering inspiration was perceived, it was revealed to me that by the will of God's dignity and purity, the accomplishment of peace is sure to be accomplished. Specifically, with nothing to hold back, the promise of complete freedom from the emotional state of want and unhappiness.

4. Aeon Giving Aeon

Once I was aware of God's trait of an immeasurable mind, I became aware of God's will to be an encouraging spirit, which endows the power of God's faith. This characteristic was specifically defined as "Aeon Giving Aeon," which is derived from God's powerful faith principles.

Characteristically, God developed the will to encourage the principles of His faith as the act of spreading His infinite power. Through the inspiration I received from the perception of God's character, I began to behave in a like manner. For the purpose of intentionally becoming as a light that shines the empowering perception of God's faith.

5. Life Giving Life

After my awareness of God's Aeon Giving Aeon trait, I then became aware of God's trait to lovingly endow the sure health of life. In a sense, this principle of God's character revealed God's defined nature of complete freedom from misery. Willfully behaving in the manner to endow His sure health of complete joy and peace.

To be specific, this trait defines God as the essence of life who willfully gives the nature of life to all outside of His Spirit. Therefore, this principle inspired in me the will to spread the health of life's joy, and peace to all I come into contact with.

6. Blessedness Giving Blessed

Consequently, once I became fully aware of God's trait of willfully sharing the health of His

Spirit, I then became aware of God's trait of sharing the prosperity of His happiness by inspiring freedom from our misery. As I acknowledged this trait, I was inspired to abide by a will to encourage the emotional prosperity of happiness by the nature of my character.

In other words, I became inspired to never intentionally be the cause of any miserable effects, but instead to cause joy and the prosperity of peace.

7. Knowledge Giving Knowledge

Once I became fully aware of God's principle to willfully encourage His prosperity of peace, I perceived His trait of expressively inspiring His faith's knowledge. Because of the revelation that I received, I was inspired to behave in the manner of obedience to the principles of God's Spirit with the intent of spreading the knowledge of God's faith through a shining character.

8. Goodness Giving Goodness

Then, as I became fully aware of God's principle to inspire the knowledge of His faith, I became aware of His trait of inspiring the goodness of His notion. This character trait defines God Spirit of Knowledge to be of a sastifing faith.

Specifically, this character trait revealed God's nature to willfully share the satisfying form of intelligence that developed His nature of complete joy and peace.

9. Mercy and Redemption Giving Mercy

Afterwards, I became aware of God's merciful nature trait, which includes His will to redeem us from the effects of misery that dwells outside of His Spirit. This trait reveals that God behaves in a lenient and compassionate manner with the intent of freeing anyone from the burdening emotions of want and unhappiness.

10. Grace Giving Grace

"However, once I came to know the finalizing principle of God Spirit, I came to understand that collectively the notion of God Character developed to be as the Source of complete joy and peace. Therefore, by being the Supreme spirit that naturally prove to be the creator of the nurture of absolute joy and peace, consequently, this supreme spirit acquired the title God. The reason being, that by the essence of God, the notion of God character suitably creates a supreme subject for worship. That is, an infinite notion for the manifestation of an eternal emotional health of absolute joy and peace."

I also came to understand that God's Spirit is the source of life, complete joy, and eternal peace, and that is what I strive for.

1 John 1:5

This then is the message which we have heard of him, and declare unto you, that God is light, and in him is no darkness at all.

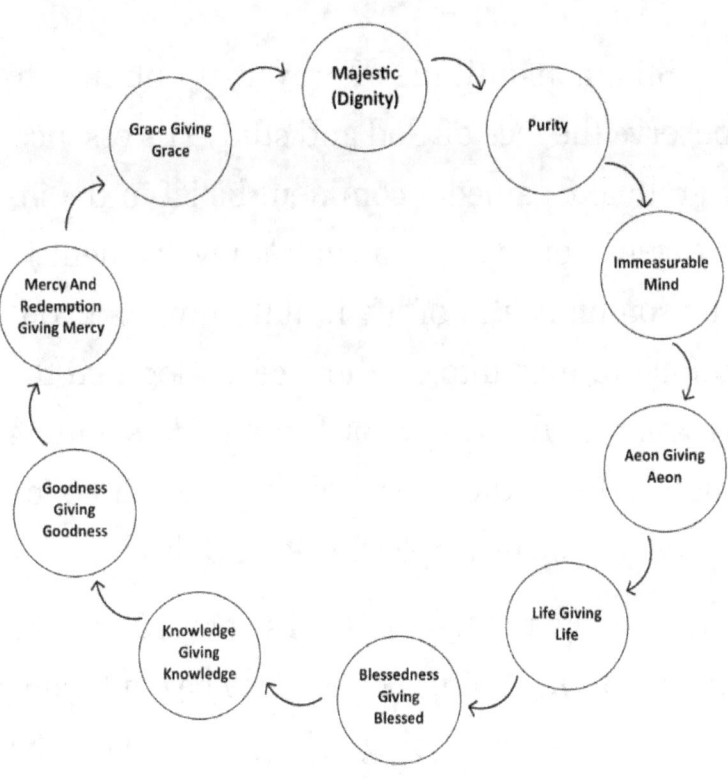

The Holy Spirit

Still in an attitude of prayer, I continued to observe the face of God and study His essence. I gradually gained a confident belief in the intelligence of the Immaculate's involvement in the soulful health of life in full form. As I continued to meditate on the face of God and the creation of the Holy Spirit, my understanding increased as the Holy Spirit revealed to be drawn by the principles of God's Spirit.

So while the light of God's character shone grace into my spirit, His essence began to amplify my understanding. I began to sense the origin of my soul, the will embedded within our creation, and the thought of how all souls are supposed to nourish and naturally live.

Collectively, as the body of God's creation, the Holy Spirit appears to be the substance evolved by the perceptive principles of God's will and knowledge. As a result, the creation of God's Holy Spirit manifested in the form of a body that emits the revelation of wisdom regarding the instructed thought of God's manner.

However, the Holy Spirit appears as a body of moral instructions and the structure of fundamental subjects that covers the entire notion of life. Therefore, appearing to be in the form of a mental arrangement pure in detail, regarding.

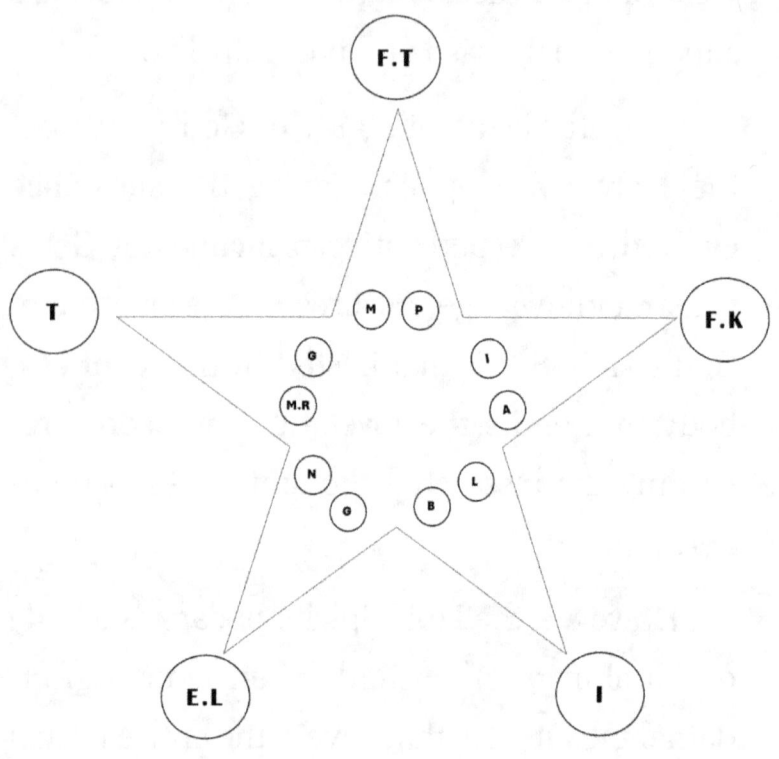

Forethought

To begin illustrating the essential being of the Holy Spirit, the initial fundamental subject to be drawn into creation is the moral revealer of forethought. For instance, this voicing light of moral instruction reveals being drawn to creation by the good perception of God's majestic nature of dignity and His will for knowledge of purity.

Therefore, in conclusion, I learned to see the first characteristic of the Holy Spirit as the revealing light that instructs the modest nature of thought, specifically regarding the guidelines of dignity and purity.

Foreknowledge

Next, as the second fundamental subject to formulate, the moral revelator of fore-knowledge evolves into creation. This moral instructing light of foreknowledge is specifically formulated by the illuminating principles of God's aspect of an immeasurable belief and His principle of being an encouraging statute of faith. In conclusion, this subject formulated as the moral revealer of manners, as the light that educates the morals of behavior as a perceived act of knowledge beforehand in regard to the principles of God's manner of an immeasurable belief and the will to behave in the obedient nature of faith.

Indestructibility

The next subject of moral instruction to formulate accordingly evolves by the aspects of God's principles to share the essence of life along with the intentional will to inspire the prosperity of God's nature of joy. This third subject is an empowering revealer of the moral instruction for an indestructible outcome of peace. Therefore, it revealed to me the enlightened blueprint for the achievement of a secure rest of peace. To conclude this character trait of the Holy Spirit, this moral revealed delivers the instruction of how to gain peace among the soul in an indestructible manner.

Eternal Life

The next characteristic to evolve reveals the empowering moral instructor of eternal life.

This subject suitably speaks in an enlightening manner, revealing the moral instructions for behavior in regard to receiving the secure outcome of eternal life.

This voice of eternal life is specifically extracted from the principles of encouraging God's knowledge by character along with the principles of inspiring the goodness of God's intelligence by behavior. Therefore, as the trait of this subject, this moral instructor emanates the teachings of how to achieve the state of eternal freedom from the emotional state of want and unhappiness. That is the eternal health of life, complete joy, and peace.

Truth

Next, as the last subject to develop, the fifth characteristic of moral instruction reveals itself as the empowering light of truth. Specifically, this subject evolves from the principles of God's merciful will to redeem by a lenient, compassionate character.

Furthermore, God's knowledge for showing undeserved mercy for the will of divine influence. So, therefore, as these two principles formulate the educating light of truth accordingly, they emit the empowering revelation of the moral instruction of how to fulfill the will of God by character.

All in all, while I came to know the body of the Holy Spirit, it then appeared in a sense that the fifth and concluding trait fulfilled the created ability of the Holy Spirit. That is completing the essential power to manifest everything that evolves into the kingdom of heaven within the fullness of God's spirit.

Therefore, in conclusion, because of the revelation I perceived, I grew to see the Holy Spirit as the moral revealer of manners that transforms the essence of another's character into the fullness of reflecting God's spiritual nature.

The Origin of Sorrow

I then received a sense of a missional purpose pertaining to souls. Through the observation of God's corresponding womb, I perceived that the intentions behind God's creation are specifically for the manifesting of His spiritual nature of life, that is, to work toward the fulfillment of manifesting freedom from all forms of misery upon the earth.

While the revelation began to settle, it all began to make perfect sense, as I recalled that we are all made in God's image (Genesis 1:27).

Along with the task to fill the earth and subdue it (Genesis 1:28). I came to see that, as the reflection of God's image, the notions of souls are naturally made to reflect the inspiring nature of God's encouraging will.

Furthermore, while also filling the earth with perceptions of faith pertaining to God's principles of character. Therefore, while doing so, we would be calming the nature of the earth through the instructive inspirations of our character.

However, it still seemed as if something was missing, so I continued to pray for clarity about our created purpose. Gradually, I came to realize that the reason why the origin of our creation was experiencing misery instead of a prolific rest was because a destructive nature had come between us and God. Consequently, the notion of souls is left in a state of confusion which leads to the destruction of peace brought about by a lack of knowledge of the commanding principles of our God.

Prayerfully, I began to wonder about how this could have happened, and instantly, my spirit became drawn to the remembrance of the story of Adam and Eve. They were specifically in a state of peace, but not yet in the manner of fulfilling their purpose; however, the two souls lost without a complete understanding of God's will. Ignorantly, they ended up allowing the nurture of destruction to encourage them to conceive a concept of misery.

Genesis 3:4-6

4 Then the serpent said to the woman, "You will not surely die. 5 For God knows that in the day you eat of it your eyes will be opened, and you will be like God, knowing good and evil." 6 So when the woman saw that the tree was good for food, that it was pleasant to the eyes, and a tree desirable to make one wise, she took of its fruit and ate. She also gave to her husband with her, and he ate.

This concept embedded the sickness of confusion in the genealogy of our soul's conscience. Specifically where the Holy Spirit is meant to dwell. However, as the understanding of this revelation began to settle in the conscience of my spirit, my focus became attracted to the awareness of Revelation 12:15–17.

Revelation 12:15-17

15 So the serpent spewed water out of his mouth like a flood after the woman, that he might cause her to be carried away by the flood. 16 But the earth helped the woman, and the earth opened its mouth and swallowed up the flood which the dragon had spewed out of his mouth. 17 And the dragon was enraged with the woman, and he went to make war with the rest of her offspring, who keep the commandments of God and have the testimony of Jesus Christ.

In a sense, the tree of the knowledge of good and evil began to appear to be the manifestation of the will of an ill-intended spirit aiming to get rid of the Holy Spirit. The reason is that the supreme evil spirit knew that the Holy Spirit was to dissolve its ability to empower the infliction of misery, resulting in destroying its evil nature.

When the supreme evil spirit attempted to dissolve the Holy Spirit by washing away God's moral instructor, the tree of knowledge of good and evil consequently sprouted among the earth. Meanwhile, the chief misery inflicting spirit descended into the earth and pursued to lure the origin of humanity into conceiving a false form of the Holy Spirit as a misguiding instructor.

As a result of the evil spirit's madness, it has wounded the natural notion of the soul's intellect into reflecting the serpent's evil commands of self-sabotaging knowledge and thieving away a part of heaven as he (the serpent) engages in war against the offspring of God and his corresponding womb. However, thereafter, my spirit then became drawn to the acknowledgment of Revelation 12:1.

Revelation 12:1

Now a great sign appeared in heaven: a woman clothed with the sun, with the moon under her feet, and on her head a garland of twelve stars.

Then as I envisioned the Holy Spirit the revelation of the creation of Christ began to be revealed.

Christ

For instance, while I was observing the revelation of God and His corresponding womb, the sight of my spirit opened up, and I saw how the emanating essence of God had shone the inspiration of an idea into His corresponding womb.

Consequently, the idea revealed to be of a child who will suitably reveal the moral instructing perceptions of God's principles by character. Furthermore, while also accordingly inspiring the growth of the Holy Spirit's seals of moral instruction.

To be more specific, the appearance of Christ revealed to me as the concept formed by the notion of the will of God's Spirit, the doctrine of the thought of God's Holy Spirit, and the inspiration of the life of God's nature, therefore concluding to be an enlightening, encouraging, and inspirational light of character that consequently supplies the nutrients of life. That is the knowledge of how to achieve the health of life and maintain it.

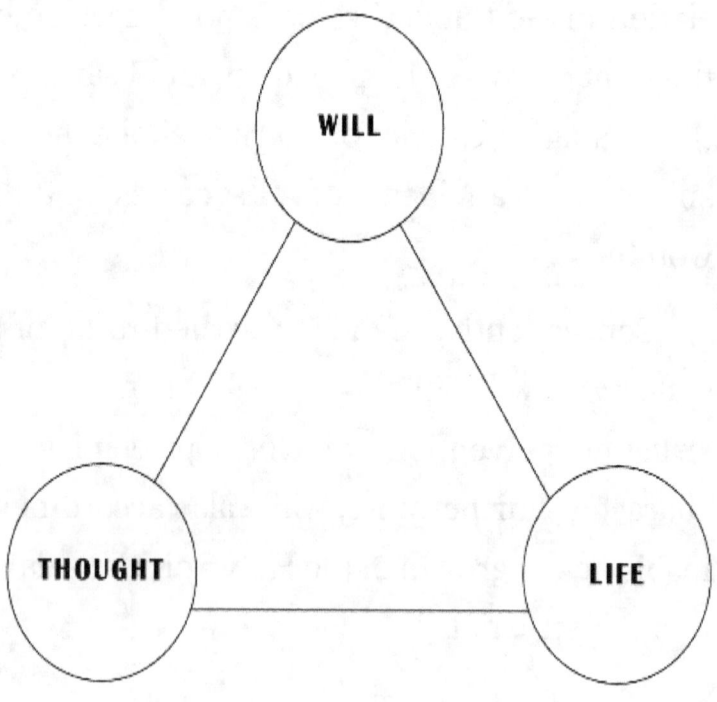

- **Will**: The notion to replenish and subdue the earth by a graceful manner and emission to emanate divine influence.

- **Thought**: The doctrine of intellectually having the intentional desire to manifest the will of God by character in an emissive manner.

- **Life**: The inspirational nature of complete salvation as an emotional health of complete joy and peace.

However, while acknowledging the revelations of Christ, I then became enlightened with the perception of the power behind how Christ specifically supplies the nutrients of life. That is His gifted ability to successfully enlighten the will of God, encourage the wisdom of God's thought, as well as inspire the health of God's nature. Therefore, the whole revelation unveiled the essence of Christ to be gifted with the power of grace, perception, understanding, and prudence.

To be specific, the powers revealed to be formed inadvertently by the concepts of knowledge. That is regarding the knowledge of God's spiritual will, the knowledge of the Holy Spirit's form of thought, and the knowledge of the nature of God's Spirit. Therefore, the revelation of the concepts of knowledge within the powers of Christ was then unveiled specifically as the character traits of Christ's Spirit. That concludes the total of 12 traits.

The Power of Grace

To begin explaining the revelation I received of Christ's character I first present the revelation of Christ's power of grace. Consequently, Christ's power of grace inspires the nutrients of life through the concept of God's spiritual will of grace.

The Power of Grace's Concepts of Knowledge

- **Will-Grace**: This first trait inspires the enlightenment of the spiritual will of God. Specifically, this trait of grace reveals the possession of the conceived notion of God's Spirit. Therefore, reflectively inspiring the enlightenment of God's spiritual will to live by the idea of grace.

- **Thought-Truth**: The second trait accordingly inspires the encouragement of knowledge regarding the Holy Spirit's thought manner. Therefore, it inspires the courage to behave in an impartial, lenient, and compassionate manner for the will of Divine influence.

- **Life-Form**: This third trait accordingly inspires the perception of a nature fully free from the defiling trait of condemnation. Therefore inspiring the idea of achieving the nature of a life that is free from the burdening notion of condemnation.

The Power of Perception

The Power of Perception's Concepts of Knowledge

This second power of Christ reveals His ability to inspire the nutrients of life by the means of enabling a conception of faith. That is, in other words, Christ's power of perception emanates the endowment of knowledge of an idea regarding the notion of God, for the purpose of memorizing God's notion of life.

- **Will-Conception**: Christ's fourth trait enlightens the will of possessing the idea of God's spiritual notion. Therefore, inspiring one to behave in a manner that accordingly reveals the possession of a notion. That is the conceived knowledge of the will of God's Spirit.

- **Thought-Perception**: This fifth trait of Christ accordingly encourages the inspiration of behavior for the means of conception. That is, in other words, inspiring the thought

of an intellectual manner of behavior. Therefore, encouraging the knowledge of behavior
regarding the notion of God's Spirit For the
means of being conceived.

- **Life-Memory**: This sixth character trait of
Christ reveals to me the health of possessing
the seals of understanding. That is regarding
God's infinite inspiring notion of life. Consequently, this trait inspires the nature of God
being gifted with a stable, conceived notion
that is the intelligence of God's Spirit.

The Power of Understanding

The power of understanding unveiled
Christ's ability to endow the knowledge of what
God's notion of life truly means. Therefore, as
the conclusion, Christ's third power reveals the
nutrients of clarity in regard to the meaning of
God's spiritual will of life.

The Power of Understanding

Concepts of Knowledge

- **Will-Understanding**: This seventh character trait of Christ enlightened the possession of Christ's Spirit, fully being aware of the means of God's spiritual nature of life as well as the spiritual nature of death (misery). Therefore, enlightening the will of knowing what God's notion of life truly means for the will of God's Spirit.

- **Thought-Love**: This eighth trait of Christ inspires the encouraging thought of God's Holy Spirit to behave in an understood manner of mercy, along with the intent to redeem. That is the inspiration of courage to behave in a lenient and compassionate manner, by the will to redeem others from the burden of misery's notion of condemnation.

- **Life-Idea**: This ninth trait of Christ inspires the perception of a nature bestowed with a plan of action regarding the understood will of God's Spirit.

The Power of Prudence

As the fourth and final power of Christ, the power of prudence emanates wisdom. In other words, this power of prudence emanates the knowledge that empowers the wise manner of God's nature.

- **The power of prudence is concepts of knowledge.**

- **Will-Perfection**: This tenth trait reveals God's notion of being without fault in regard to His will to manifest peace. Therefore, Christ's tenth trait inspires the will of perfection by enlightening the intentional principle of willfully not being the cause of any misery aroused specifically for the will of perfection, the manifestation of peace.

- **Thought-Peace**: This eleventh trait of Christ encourages the thought to live in a calm order for the means of producing the fulfillment of a nature that is free from all warring disturbances. Therefore, this trait of

Christ concludes to enlighten the will of maintaining and producing a happily calm nature by the tools of behavior. In other words for the means of manifesting the fullness of God's spiritual nature of freedom from all misery.

- **Life-Wisdom**: The twelfth and concluding trait of Christ inspires the gift of discernment regarding the understanding of God's will. That is, in other words, Christ's spiritual trait of wisdom has proved to reveal the nature of healthfully being gifted with the understanding of God's will as well as the discernment of how to fulfill the will of God's Spirit.

In summary, Christ's trait of wisdom inspires the gift of being a prolific mindset of discernment. That is, in a sense, the gift of possessing the guidance of God's spiritual principles for the achieved outcome of joy and peace.

However, in conclusion to the entire revelation of Christ, the Spirit of Christ revealed to be an empowering light that endows the affections of faith.

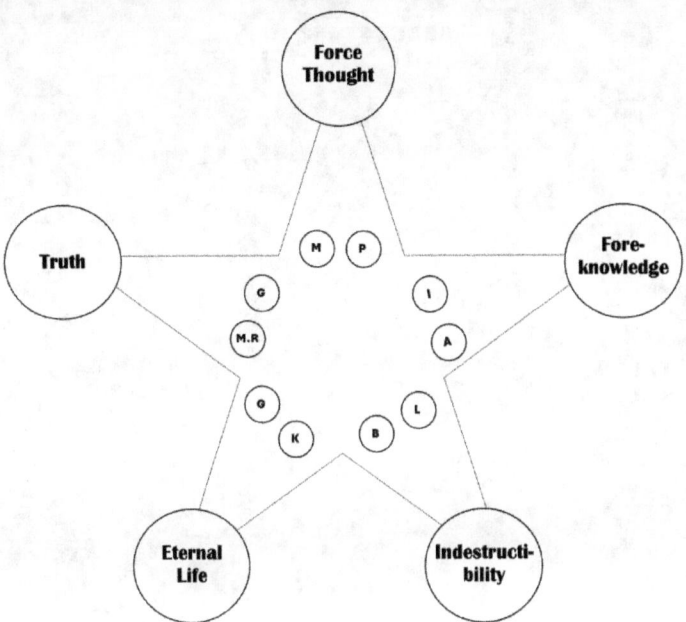

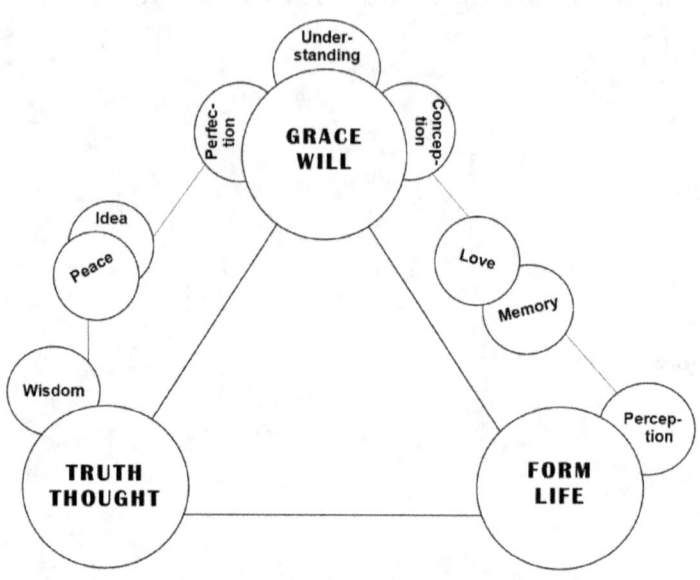

Persuasion

Once I became fully aware of the exact powers of Christ, I couldn't help but begin wondering why God deliberately held back the gift of Christ until the time when He formed the flesh of Jesus Christ, for if the notion of humanity had been endowed with the light of Christ, the notion of souls would have never had to experience the burden of misery.

Yet, by an epiphany, inevitably, I began to recognize that through my time of not knowing who Christ was, as well as having the absence of the Holy Spirit, the lifestyle of frustration, pain, and misery drew my heart into desiring the gift of faith even more. Therefore, due to my unfortunate circumstances, my belief in an actual Savior and a redeeming faith became profoundly established. as well as my affectionate need for a new train of thought for the purpose of rebirthing the peace of my life.

Furthermore, I realized that, through my desperateness, the results of my unintelligent sin undoubtably chastised me into opening my eyes and actually seeing that the essence of God's Spirit is what I truly needed in order to receive a stable, complete life of peace.

However, because I was finally getting to know Christ prolifically, I came to receive the affections of God's faith. And I also began to receive mental seals of understanding, which gradually settled in my spirit as a profound transformation of thought. Therefore, while I was receiving the gifts of understanding and affection, I also grew to see how Christ's spirit persuades a soul's heart into accepting the covenants of God's Spirit.

For instance, these covenants would inspirationally come in the form of affections, and define the receiving of God's knowledge in order to be fulfilled with the joy of God's prosperity and peace. These affections become encouraged within a person's heart, as the acknowledged need for the knowledge of God, for the salvation of life.

I eventually realized that these affections were derived from three major cycles of experience. In other words, by these particular cycles of life, the fullness of God's love within develops by receiving the knowledge of God in an obeying manner, by the experience of three major character shaping genre of circumstances in life. More precisely, these genre proved to be the test of faith, the test of endurance, and the test of hope.

Thus, these kinds of situations will test our soul's loving obedience to the acknowledged principles of God. These tests will demonstrate if a person genuinely heeds God's teachings and conceives His knowledge in the sense of trust and faith.

However, as these three types of circumstances challenge a soul's heart accordingly, they will aim to build the soul's character into the likeness of Christ. That is, only if the soul allows God's chastising love to do so. Therefore, for my next chapter, I would like to share with you the revealed knowledge of God's seven covenants, which connect the soul of humankind to the nature of God's kingdom of complete joy and peace.

Covenant Affections

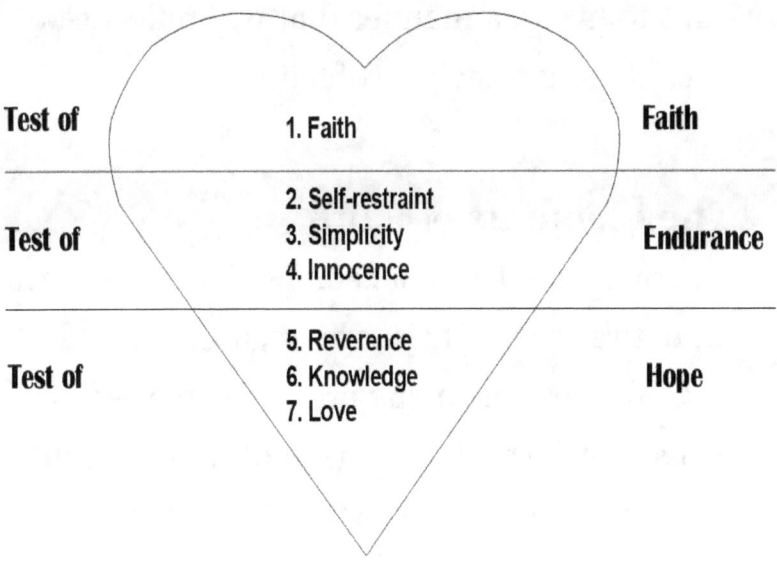

Test of		Faith
	1. Faith	
Test of	2. Self-restraint 3. Simplicity 4. Innocence	Endurance
Test of	5. Reverence 6. Knowledge 7. Love	Hope

Faith

Throughout my experience of getting to know God, His Holy Spirit, and His Christ, I have learned to see that through the natural frustration of life, God is intentionally presenting to a soul the teachings of faith. Therefore, as the affections of faith that God works to build within our hearts, God's chastisement will specifically be for the affectionate conception of God's life guiding principles of dignity, purity, immeasurable belief, and the accepted covenant to live in a manner that will reflect God's encouraging principles of faith.

The Elements of Faith

An element is a substance that helps form an entire thing. Therefore, regarding the faith of God, these elements are the perceived concepts that form the doctrine of faith, which is the actual blueprint of what the faith of God is made of.

Dignity

For starters, the first element in the covenant of faith evolves as the affectionate belief to live in the majestic manner of dignity. Specifically, this element of faith evolves from the desire for salvation, and in return, it develops as the conceived affection to live cautiously to avoid arousing the nature of misery upon my own soul.

Purity

This second element of faith is regarding the submissive acceptance of the obedient nature of God's principle of purity. Specifically, this element evolves as the received affection to not be the cause of any misery evolves outside of the nature of self. In other words, it is the conceived affection of the aspect for living purely for the perfection of peace.

Immeasurable Belief

This next element is specifically presented by the challenge of fear, which is the expectation of the nature of misery. However, through the tests and trials that God presents to a soul, He aims to teach us the immeasurable power of His Spirit. That is regarding the intelligence of God's living principles.

Hence, the element of immeasurable belief is the growth of believing that the achievement of stable, eternal peace is confidently possible to achieve through obedience to God's principles of dignity and purity.

Aeon

An "Aeon" is a supreme power that flows out of a manifesting power. So therefore, when a soul receives God's aspect to characterly reflect the Principles of God Spirit, accordingly, that soul would begin to flow out of that same inspiring supreme power of God.

Therefore, this element of affectionate change, suitably develops by the challenge of action. That is, when God presents the test of life for the reasons of encouraging an actual, exterted character change.

Hebrews 11:1

Now faith is the substance of things hoped for, the evidence of things not seen.

In conclusion, these four elements of dignity, purity, immeasurable belief, and Aeon collide as an affectionate train of thought. That of which is a perceived and instructed manner of how to achieve the nature of God's peace and prosperity of joy.

As the substance of things hoped for, these four elements evolved to be the affectionately conceived intelligence of God's Spirit. That is as

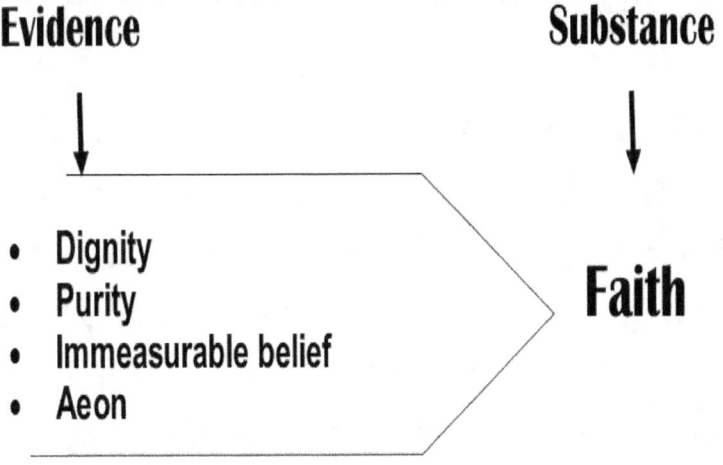

Evidence   **Substance**

- Dignity
- Purity
- Immeasurable belief
- Aeon

Faith

a belief for a hope of peace that accordingly manifests as the expected outcome of faith.

Endurance

This next genre of character building circumstances is the genre of endurance. To experience endurance specifically means to sustain challenging circumstances without yielding to a defiled form of faith. However, as a result of enduring, the development of three new affectionate aspects takes place as the affectionate submittance to a covenant with God. Therefore, specifically, these next three covenants are the agreed concept of faith in regard to the committed trust and the principles of God's Spirit.

Self-Restraint

This second covenant encourages its way into a praying heart is presented during frustrating times, while God aims to challenge a soul's behavior. Specifically, God would be aiming to encourage the affection of restraining oneself from falling into the temptation of neglecting the foundational principles of God's faith.

That is, for the purpose of reflecting the empowering principles of God's character in a stable manner of faith through the tempting circumstances of life. Therefore, once a soul has received the affectionate covenant of faith accordingly, God will then present the test of frustrating circumstances just to inspire the covenant of self-restraint.

Simplicity

The affection of simplicity is the conceived inspiration to live in a manner that keeps life uncomplicated. Accordingly, this covenant proves to be inspired through the testing times of temptation. Specifically, the challenge is to behave in a wise manner to avoid complications. That is, to avoid assisting the cause of misery. Therefore, the affection of simplicity settles as the agreed covenant to cautiously avoid complications regarding the obedient nature of God's wisdom.

Innocence

As the concluding covenant of the genre of endurance, the affection of innocence is the conceived inspiration to cautiously live in a manner of avoiding the defilement of guilt. In other words, it is to avoid acquiring the wage of being the cause of any misery aroused within any type of predicament.

Therefore, the affection of innocence concludes as the settled agreement to live in a wise manner of preventing the defilement of guilt. However, as the conclusion of circumstantial endurance, the covenant of self, restraint, simplicity, and innocence proves to be inspired through the trials of endurance.

Therefore, as the final outcome, these covenants reveal to be the received inspiration of submissively living by the affectionate need of God's wisdom in order to achieve the eternal nature of God's peace.

Hope

Once I understood what the experience of endurance was, the next circumstantial genre of life that a soul would enter is the phase of hope. Specifically, the phase of hope inspires the affectionate covenants of persistency regarding the manner of God's faith.

Therefore, this circumstantial genre works the development of the covenants pertaining to persistently pursuing life by the manner of God's faith, along with the confident expectation of receiving God's complete nature of joy and peace.

Reverence

As the fifth covenant of God, the affection of reverence revealed to be a conceived aspect of affectionately looking upon others with the deepest respect. That is, to treat others with special consideration. Specifically, this special consideration relates to cautiously behaving in a manner towards others for the considerate result of inspiring the tendency of God's life of complete peace.

Therefore, in conclusion, the inspiration of reverence settles as the conceived inspiration to behave in the manner of reverence for the confident expectation of achieving the peace of God.

Knowledge

The next covenant to develop by the circumstantial genre of hope is the conceived aspect to affectionately live by the knowledge of God's Spirit. To be more specific it is to confidently adopt the lenient nature and compassionate manner of God.

Specifically to abolish the nature of misery and, in return, evolve the nature of life into a complete health of joy and peace. Therefore, this covenant is the received inspiration to affectionately abide by the manner of God's knowledge for the sure expectancy of God's complete nature of joy and peace.

Love

As the seventh and concluding covenant, the affection of love is the conceived inspiration to affectionately behave in a manner of showing undeserving mercy by emanating a divine influence by character.

To be specific, the divine influence would be the enlightening encouragement of a manner that accordingly inspires the perception of God's infinite and life-giving faith. Therefore, as the completing covenant between God and the praying soul, the covenant of love is the conceived aspect of living in an influential manner for the means of complete peace to secure the confident expectation of complete eternal joy and peace.

Hebrews 10: 16

This is the covenant that I will make with them after those days, saith the Lord, I will put my laws into their hearts, and in their minds will I write them.

In summary, throughout my prayer for understanding, knowledge, and wisdom, these covenants were revealed to be as the written mutual agreements between the Spirit of God and praying souls.

Specifically, these covenants prove to be. The arrangement of God's spirit. Written on the table of a receiving soul's heart. In the form of affection. Therefore, these covenants reveal themselves to be as submissive agreement to commit to the principles of God's spirit by way of entering and engaging to fulfill the will of God's spirit by character for the means of a prolific rest.

From God to You

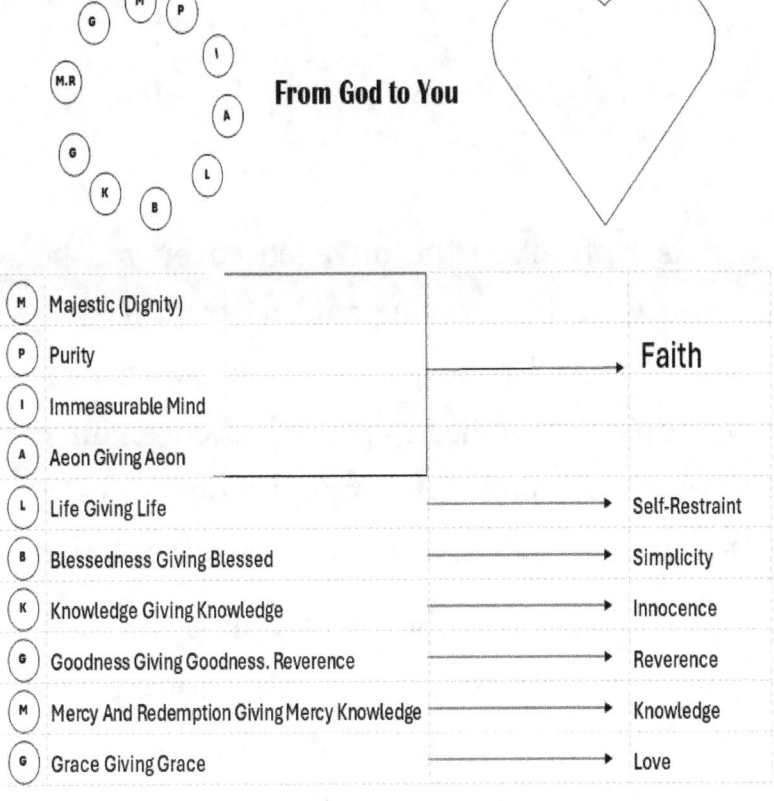

From God to You

M	Majestic (Dignity)		
P	Purity		Faith
I	Immeasurable Mind		
A	Aeon Giving Aeon		
L	Life Giving Life	→	Self-Restraint
B	Blessedness Giving Blessed	→	Simplicity
K	Knowledge Giving Knowledge	→	Innocence
G	Goodness Giving Goodness. Reverence	→	Reverence
M	Mercy And Redemption Giving Mercy Knowledge	→	Knowledge
G	Grace Giving Grace	→	Love

As I observed the unveiled covenants between God and praying souls, I couldn't help but wonder why the heart. In other words, why would God specifically place His covenant in the heart of a soul? So as my spirit pondered the thought, I then began to recognize the relation.

I could see that the heart is the primary organ for a body to be alive. Therefore, as the heart operates, it will circulate the passion of the soul throughout the soul's body as a means of an operating character. Yet as the covenants between God and humankind dwell in the heart as affections, the affections would begin to circulate through the soul's body and inward persuasion to a new behavior. Then, the inward persuasion would produce a character that reflects the newly conceived notion of God's spirit.

As the heart pump's a new passion through a soul's body, that same spirit of God that renewed the soul's mind into the mutual agreement of manner would then begin to present itself through the nature of the soul's character. Then the rebirthed soul would start to enlighten the principles of God, encourage the wisdom of God's Holy Spirit, and inspire the nature of life's complete freedom from misery by character.

Therefore, this proliferation feeds the consciences of neighboring souls the nutrients of life that miserable souls have always yearned for. Furthermore, it will leave behind a legacy of infinite inspiration that will consequently dissolve the chaos of the world. So therefore, as a soul gains this blessing of prolificacy, it will gain the most value on earth, which is its fruitful purpose of subduing and replenishing the earth with the good fruits of life.

Epilogue

While I finally got to know God, I became aware of how our souls are in a sense, a breath from God. Although as breathes from God, we are instantly born into the chastising circumstances of life, which I have learned to see as the teachings of God.

In a sense, I strongly believe that if God had not blown us into the chastising hardness of life, we would have never grown to understand the value of where we are birthed from, which is the Spirit of God. Therefore, as God blew us into creation, not only did He craft the infant cry for life within the sense of our souls, but He also blew us into creation as a prayer of His own.

So as I grew to see how souls are the off-spring of God, I also became aware of how we are God's prayer to fill the earth with the light of His Spirit, which would manifest the prolification of calming the earth from all evil as well as filling the earth with the essence of God's inspiring Spirit.

It is hard to avoid the fact that we only suffer misfortunate circumstances because we have not learned the sure way of life. Yet once we have achieved this sure way of life, it proves to manifest the blessings of God's peace, specifically because we have grown into the maturity of fulfilling our creative purpose. With this being said, I pray I have enlightened, encouraged, and inspired you into achieving the blessed path of a prolific prayer.

The Prolific Prayer

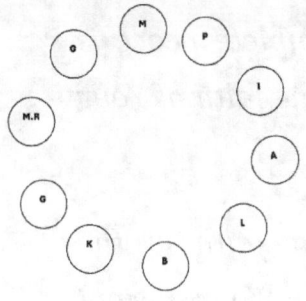

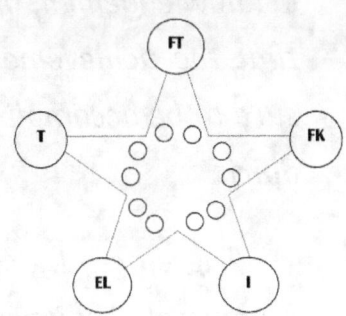

- Majestic (Dignity)
- Immeasurable Mind
- Life Giving Life
- Knowledge Giving Knowledge
- Mercy And Redemption Giving Mercy

- Purity
- Aeon Giving Aeon
- Blessedness Giving Blessed
- Goodness Giving Goodness
- Grace Giving Grace

- Fore-Thought
- Fore-Knowledge
- Indestructibility
- Eternal Life
- Truth

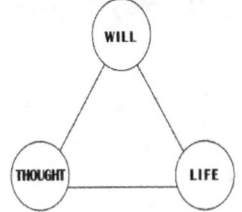

Will	Thought	Life
Grace	Truth	Form
Conception	Perception	Memory
Understanding	Love	Idea
Perfection	Peace	Wisdom

- Faith
- Simplicity
- Reverence

- Self-Restraint
- Innocence
- Knowledge

- Love

God, I acknowledge Your dignity, and I acknowledge Your purity. And through the acknowledgement of Your nature, I prioritize that the achievement of complete peace is sure to be accomplished by the faith of Your Spirit.

Therefore, I accept Your faith in the manner of obedience. I worship Your spirit of life by earnestly inspiring Your nature by my character.

I affectionately agree to obey Your will to encourage the prosperity of Your spiritual happiness, and I commit to Thy faith for the means of enlightening knowledge that will bring sure peace.

God, I also agree to willfully encourage the goodness of Thy nature through my behavior, and I commit to Thy will to show mercy and a lenient and compassionate manner for the will to help pull other souls out of the miserable depths of unhappiness.

I submit to behave in an impartial manner for the will of presenting the divine influence of Thy faith.

Therefore, I thank You for the gift of Your modest forethought. I thank You for the gift of Your diligent foreknowledge. I thank You for the gift of Your guiding voice for the means of an indestructible peace.

Thank You for the gift of Your guiding voice for the means of achieving the eternal nature of life. And I thank You for the gift of Your instructing spirit that guides me in the truth of Your manner.

So now, God. I trust in You with all faith. I trust in You and your suggestion of self-restraint. I trust in Your doctrine of simplicity. I trust in Your idea of innocence.

Affectionately, I also submit to Your manner of reverence, and I submit to Your will of presenting Your spiritual knowledge through my character. Therefore, I commit to

Your will to show undeserved mercy with the intent of divine influence, so that I may complete the task of achieving a prolific prayer.

About The Author

 Brandon Tyrelle Chambers discovered his love for writing and prayer after experiencing several life-changing events at a young age. He was traveling the United States as a well-known musician before his life suddenly changed in a way he could never imagine. He suffered tremendous losses.

After being incarcerated, he discovered who God truly is. He is sharing his testimony with the world. He prays that this offering of heartfelt love for God will encourage you to establish a strong relationship with God and never let go.